AUTHORS

Chris Adams
Chris Adams is a consultant, designer, and speaker with 20-plus years of experience helping clients engage people, processes, and technology to improve performance. He writes the Performance Consulting Tips blog series on TD.org.

Beth Hughes
Beth Hughes has more than 18 years of experience in designing and developing learning solutions. She focuses on developing curriculum-level programs with comprehensive, blended learning designs.

Content Manager, Instructional Design
Eliza Blanchard, APTD

Editor, *TD at Work*
Patty Gaul

Managing Editor
Joy Metcalf

Graphic Designer
Shirley E.M. Raybuck

COPYRIGHT © ATD

Learning professionals know the value of learning— it's importance and how powerful it can be. But how do you show the value of your work and demonstrate the value of L&D activities to the organizations you serve?

That question, a common topic of discussion among learning consultants, spurred us to write this issue of *TD at Work*. In an attempt to show the value of our own work, we reviewed projects we've completed during the past five years to identify which ones stakeholders perceived as most valuable during and after the work. This review changed our conversation: Instead of asking ourselves, "How can we demonstrate the value of learning to the organization?" we began to ask a more fundamental question: "How can we be more valuable to the organization?"

Compare these opposite experiences as a learning consultant: developing a one-hour e-learning course describing this year's policy updates and designing a comprehensive set of experiences that increase client retention by 30 percent within three months.

When we create learning content that companies value, we benefit personally. Meaningful work is a fuel that powers the quality of what we produce, the effort we extend, and our ownership of the outcomes. It is disheartening to produce training programs that accomplish no more than checking a box for learners and their supervisors. Consultants who connect real operational results with their work elevate their performance from acceptance to enthusiasm, a virtuous cycle where organizational value and personal purpose drive each other.

Learning consultants often attempt to prove the value of learning programs after their completion through evaluation, measurement, or analytics. These tools can help demonstrate changes in an organization. But for those changes to be meaningful, before you even consider learning programs, you need to give them context by defining the goals the company needs to accomplish. Rather than prove the value of a completed product, be a valuable partner with every action you take. Grab opportunities to insert value during the process—these are infinitely greater and much more meaningful. Be more valuable by:
- aligning work with organizational goals to produce real results
- curating learning experiences that cultivate change leaders
- creating mutually beneficial partnerships with your clients based upon open communication and collaboration.

A distinguishing factor between projects that checked off a box and projects that noticeably affected learner behavior and organizational outcomes was a focus on results during every phase of the project. This was not just as a post-implementation afterthought but from the first project discovery meeting on. The key differentiator is that results come first.

In this issue of *TD at Work*, we'll:
- Introduce the Results Come First framework.
- Describe how results should come first when learning consultants engage with clients.
- Caution about forces that may throw off the balance of your development initiative.
- Provide an example of how the framework works in action.

The Results Come First Framework

The Results Come First framework is comprised of five elements that are depicted along a parallel track. Each element has three associated sub-elements or factors. The flow between elements is unique in that it operates in either direction, depending on where and how the framework is applied. Before we discuss how the elements flow together, let's define each.

Organizational Results

Organizational results are tangible business results that a company needs to achieve to remain successful over time. Numbers describe those results. For the purposes of the framework, a firm may be for-profit, nonprofit, or governmental. Organizations may also function within a larger entity; for example, a region or department of a company may be an organization.

Figure 1. Results Come First Framework

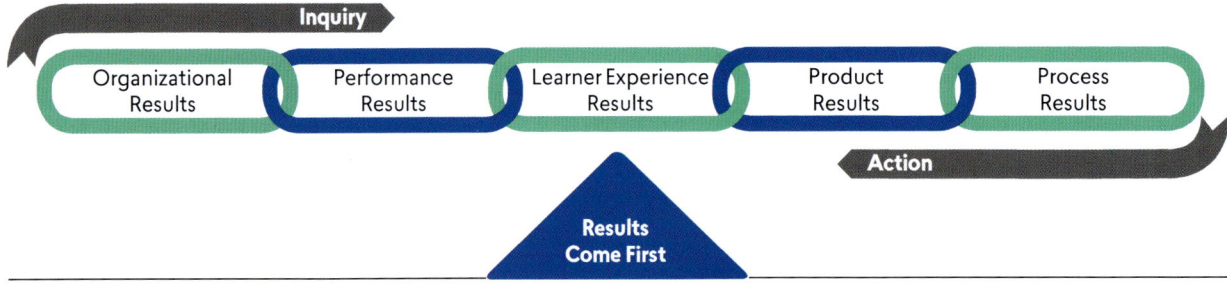

© 2019 Chris Adams and Beth Hughes. Reprinted with permission.

The three factors of this element, which represent the most common categories in which these results fall, are:
- cost—reducing or managing costs
- revenue—increasing or generating revenue
- compliance—meeting business operating standards or requirements.

Performance Results

Moving into the framework, the next element is performance results. Note that each element is linked as the framework proceeds, so these are the performance results learners or organization members must accomplish to produce the organizational results.

Performance results are evidenced on the job via a group of learners' behaviors and are measured in terms of accomplishments. Author, psychologist, and founder of performance technology Thomas Gilbert stresses that behavior is what you can see someone do in the moment, but accomplishment is what stays behind when the individual leaves. For example, you can see a sales rep interacting with a customer, but it is the closed sale receipt that is left after the call.

Factors related to performance results fall into these subcategories:
- behavior change—increasing, decreasing, or modifying behavior
- time to proficiency—decreasing time to proficiency on the job
- advocacy—learners promoting behavior change to others and becoming change leaders.

Learner Experience Results

Experience here is inclusive of both instructional and non-instructional solution components. The internal change that takes place within each learner is important, but equally important may be the changes to learners' environment that remove barriers or provide support in them achieving the required performance results. Those are the desired results for the learners' experience as a whole.

Learning experience factors include:
- capability—learners acquiring knowledge and skills
- engagement—learners grasping relevance and being motivated to continue learning
- experience—learners gaining a certain experience (for example, working within different cultural contexts) that support future performance.

Product Results

Learning experience design is ultimately about specifying, selecting, building, and implementing learning products. Over time, companies have come to expect more and more from their learning products. Multiple goals for these products have been overlaid. It is no longer sufficient to produce effective instruction. Leaders now often expect learning products to engage, entertain, and inspire—factors that you must take into consideration.

As such, learning product results factors are:
- quality—meeting quality standards
- novelty—introducing innovations
- marketability—generating buzz and demand.

Process Results

The Results Come First framework is meant to be applicable to many instructional design or development models. Whether it's a more traditional approach similar to ADDIE (analysis, design, development, implementation, and evaluation), Agile, or the Successive Approximation Model, designers of learning products and learner experiences employ a process in their work.

The process results element considers the stakeholder experience. Often, we find that if clients or project sponsors are not pleased with the design process, they are predisposed to see the products of that design in a negative light.

The categories of factors that relate to the process results elements are:
- time—meeting timeline requirements
- budget—meeting budget requirements
- relationship—establishing or building relationships among the project team.

How Results Come First

The Results Come First framework is not a new model for creating effective instruction or a new process for designing relevant training materials. Rather, it is an approach we have developed with the intent of shifting the mindset of those in the organization who are responsible for learning from a focus on deliverables to a focus on results. Within this framework, you identify the desired results for a training initiative up front and then maintain a purposeful focus on those results through the project's course. This focus change more closely aligns learning initiatives with business and performance goals.

Collaborating With Clients

Using this framework, begin your efforts by identifying the desired results for the work of all stakeholders involved in the project, such as the client or project sponsor, the project team, and the learners. This requires stakeholders to clearly define what they mean by *results*, in measurable terms, for the given initiative. During this stage, partner with your client to identify the desired results across different dimensions to ensure that learning solutions are closely aligned with the client's business and performance goals. A collaborative approach is essential—use the framework to help your clients consider all factors that could contribute to project success, creating a complete and realistic picture of the targeted changes.

Clients may be surprised when this work reveals desired outcomes they had not originally identified or expressed in their initial training request or project objectives. For example, a content provider may provide a training request with a stated goal of training staff to more effectively attract new clients to increase its client base. After a thorough inquiry into the desired results, you may find that a more valuable outcome would be increasing product sales within the current client base by building the staff's skills in making referrals.

Experience with the framework has shown that this provides immediate value to the client by clarifying the results it expects to achieve up front, which immediately improves work products because they are designed to target these future outcomes.

While the Results Come First framework enables the project team to identify specific, desired results across 15 factors, not all desired results can be weighted equally—clients will always value some outcomes more than others. For instance, a client may value project budget over novelty or may value learner engagement over production timeline. You can provide value to clients by helping them evaluate the identified set of desired results and balancing them in favor of those that are most important to them. That provides a context for decision making across the project.

At each decision point, ask yourself, "Does this decision align with our most important desired results?" As project work progresses, influencing factors will inevitably arise that can change priorities and require a shift in focus. For example, when handling typical project constraints such as timeline and budget or when you face unexpected challenges such as a sponsor reversing previously made decisions, ask yourself and the client that question—that helps you make choices in service of ultimate outcomes, rather than current circumstances. By first establishing distinct priorities, you can more efficiently and effectively overcome obstacles that arise, because you will have an established anchor guiding decision making through each step of the process. What clients want may shift over a project, but what they need likely won't.

Hone In on the Learner Experience

While learning consultants can act on any of the framework's elements, the learner experience is the focus of those actions. LX is the point where learning products either connect or fail to connect with desired performance. It's also the point where critical environmental factors come into play. Learning products alone are insufficient to produce changes in performance and organizational results. Learners must be appropriately compensated, equipped, informed, and supported if performance is to occur.

Experience is the point on which all other elements balance. It is also the crucial link between products and performance. Because of this, just as you must carefully craft products, you must carefully curate LX.

Change Management Framework

The Results Come First framework is a change management model at its core. It is not designed to change what learning consultants do but rather how they do it. As such, you can overlay it onto whatever instructional design model an organization may follow. The sustained focus on results that the framework provides will change the way you work during each step of the process, as well as relationships with your clients.

Think about how the framework could influence a training project completed using an Agile methodology. Each iteration of requirements and solutions would be founded on a set of identified and prioritized desired results that the entire team has confidence in. Imagine if you shifted focus from products to results in your organization—what impact do you think that change would have in your L&D function?

How the Framework Functions

The framework's elements, as discussed, are causally linked—as you move from right to left through the framework, the results of each element produce the next element. This is the *chain of action*, because enacting each element leads to the following element, creating dependencies throughout the model:

- Consultants engage in a process, which produces a set of products.
- Learners engage with products, which help shape their experience.
- Learners have an experience (or set of experiences) that drives and supports a change in their performance.
- The learners' changed performance drives and supports changes in the organization, leading to improved business outcomes.

Why, then, are the elements structured as organizational results to process results rather than process results to organizational results? As mentioned earlier, the parallel track on which the elements rest works in both directions. While the elements produce a chain of action when implemented as a solution, your work should begin in the opposite direction. This is the *chain of inquiry*, because when you first seek to understand the results that your clients or stakeholders desire, you start by asking questions as far to the left of the framework as you can. Ideally, beginning with organizational results, ask:

- What organizational results are needed for the company to be successful?
- What performance results must we achieve to produce those results?
- What experience must learners have to produce those performance results?
- What products must we specify, select, design, develop, and implement to produce that experience?
- What process does the project team (clients, stakeholders, consultants) need to experience to successfully produce those products?

> **Learning consultants can provide value to clients by helping them evaluate the identified set of desired results and balancing those in favor of results that are most important to the client.**

Just as it would be illogical to expect to produce a product without employing a process, or a chain of action, it is equally nonsensical to ask what experience you desire for learners before you understand what performance that experience is meant to produce.

Balance

During an ideal project, first use the chain of inquiry to gather data on your client's desired results and set the foundation for a trusted partnership. Then reverse direction, using the chain of action, following a process, and developing products that create a specific learner experience that supports the desired performance and organizational results. Throughout a typical project, however, do not remain fixed on one element—such as learning experience or performance. Rather, move back and forth as the project progresses, with your focus targeted on one, or maybe two, specific elements at any one time.

As you progress through the chain of inquiry, picture this focus as a weight. Focusing on the left of the framework on the organizational element gives more weight to that end of the framework. As you move through the framework, the weight of focus shifts, creating a teeter-totter or seesaw motion as the work advances.

Your ultimate goal is to evenly balance the weight across the framework so that all five elements are sufficiently cared for during the project's course. In a healthy state, or state of balance, the total weight is evenly distributed. Projects in a state of balance, overall, require less effort on your part and are more likely to produce desired results.

A state of balance is easy to achieve when you are in complete control of the effort from start to finish. However, that is rarely the case. Forces tend to arise throughout the project that influence where your

The Learning Consultant's Role

In the Results Come First framework, learning consultants who want to provide the most value to their organizations must maintain a focus on results through every phase of an L&D project. Most consultants we spoke with envisioned their role as rooted in instructional design but with a much broader perspective of training within the organization. However, several tasks differentiate a learning consultant's role from that of an instructional designer.

- **Needs assessment.** Learning consultants typically conduct needs assessments that are broader than the product level. They look at teams', organizations', and individuals' performance needs. They identify performance gaps and root causes, and their recommendations to close those gaps may be training or other solutions, depending on analysis results.
- **Relationship management.** A key differentiator of the learning consultant role is managing the relationships associated with any need. This involves relationships at all levels, such as business partners, stakeholders, clients, and instructional designers. Beyond producing quality training materials, learning consultants may help business owners recognize the value of a training solution, get buy-in from stakeholders, or give clients visibility into the process. They are responsible for taking in training requests and, often, reframing them to identify true business needs.
- **Aligning learning with business goals.** Learning consultants are responsible for producing learning programs that support business initiatives. Their solutions must not only change behavior but change behavior in service of the business needs. Their recommendations must tie directly to measurable outcomes to balance cost versus benefit. Additionally, learning consultants must continuously adjust based on shifting needs. As one learning consultant stated, "More than focusing on the learning results of an activity, I focus on what are the business results. And the closer I can tie the learning results to the business outcomes, the more successful the project is and the better buy-in I have from leaders."

Learning consultants are ultimately responsible for producing the change in employee behavior that meets the organization's business goals. They are the bridge between the business and performers, one built by the relationships they develop and manage. While many lines of business share responsibility for getting an organization from point A (a business goal) to point B (goal achievement), learning consultants take on the responsibility for the HR component. They turn strategic initiatives into tactical performance solutions through partnerships along with careful management of expectations. They deliver learning solutions rather than training products.

attention is focused at a given point in time. Two types of forces—leading and emergent—act upon the framework.

Leading Forces

Leading forces are factors known at the beginning of a project that are within your control. Still, you must address them to keep the project in a balanced state. These are areas where you place intentional added weight, based on given parameters such as business needs, performance needs, or environmental constraints. Work together with the client to evaluate these forces and selectively focus one or more elements to align with desired results.

> **Emergent forces require yours or the client's response to keep the project on track.**

Consider these scenarios of leading forces acting on organizational results:
- *The rollout of a new system is scheduled in three months, with training required prior to the go-live date.* This is a leading force acting on organizational results. To balance this force, place your focus on the process results to accelerate the work.
- *A key back-office system is being discontinued; a new system will replace it.* This is a leading force acting on the organizational results. To achieve this, place the focus on the product results—to create a training program that can produce similar performance and experience outcomes with the new system as with the old.
- *The client is providing customer training as an add-on product.* You may need to focus on establishing a methodology—that is, a process result—that meets the desired revenue for the organizational goal.

As the learning consultant, you manage the leading forces—which are known early on—by strategically building the chain at the beginning of the project. Based on known information, identify the framework elements upon which you should place intentional focus, working in agreement with your client. However, you must also distribute the remaining weight evenly across the framework for the project to be successful.

Again, picture a teeter-totter. If you place a disproportionate amount of weight on one side or the other side, that throws the framework out of balance, and you may not achieve the desired results. A focus only on product results with no reference to desired performance and organizational results is likely a waste of time and resources.

At times, an out-of-balance state is unavoidable. For instance, the client is operating within a severely constrained timeline that must be met at the expense of other elements. In such cases, make the client aware of the potential impacts. It is your role to care for each element in some way—if unequally, then intentionally so.

Emergent Forces

Emergent forces are unanticipated forces that arise during the course of the project, which add pressure to one or more framework elements. They are outside of your control and emerge as a result of previously unknown information becoming known, a change in the leading forces identified at the beginning of the project, or because you or the client didn't care properly for those leading forces to begin with. Emergent forces require yours or the client's response (or a response from both of you) to keep the project on track. For example:
- Prototype testing reveals that the designed solution is not technically compatible with the client's environment (pressure may be placed on product results).
- The client reveals a previously unexpressed business goal (pressure may be placed on organizational results).
- A key business process changes that significantly affects training content (pressure may be placed on performance results).

You must manage emergent forces by first detecting them and then balancing the chain as an ongoing effort during the project. You can typically restore balance by placing an equal focus on the opposite end of the framework—that is, counterbalancing.

Let's look at a couple of examples:
- Your client asks you to update its sales training curriculum to reflect the current market and available support tools. After you've completed the curriculum design and made recommendations for the new product, the client informs you that the company needs to reduce the instructor-led component you recommended because it does not have an instructor available to deliver it. This new information is a midproject emergent force placed on the organizational results. To address this shift, you can redesign the course to reduce in-class learner time by 40 percent. You have then responded to an unanticipated force on the desired organizational results by intentionally adjusting expectations around the desired product results.
- During production of a one-hour e-learning course on the new release of a point-of-sale (where the transaction occurs) system, the primary subject matter expert is pulled into another project, reducing availability by half. You know this is a force affecting the process results—review cycles cannot proceed as scheduled with such limited reviewer time. In response, you can place weight on the organizational element at the opposite end of the framework, reminding the client of its desired result to deliver training before the system release date in six weeks. You and the client can then take action as needed—such as by finding additional resources—to adjust the process so the targeted business goal is still achievable.

Using the Framework to Manage Forces

Your role is to manage leading and emergent forces so that they support, rather than detract from, achieving desired results. While you can proactively care for leading forces, you must respond reactively to emergent forces. The Results Come First framework provides a model for applying an initial and sustained focus on results and can help you recommend appropriate action when something threatens to throw the project off course. Furthermore, it provides a context for you to discuss the relationship between causes and potential effects with clients.

You can use the framework to demonstrate how a strategic or logistical change can directly affect other elements, risking the achievement of desired results, and collaborate to identify the best purposeful action to take. Establishing clear, desired results at the beginning of the project helps you make choices in service of ultimate outcomes, rather than current circumstances. When you work in partnership with clients to prioritize the desired results, you can more efficiently and effectively overcome obstacles that arise, because you have an established anchor guiding decision making through each step of the process. Decisions made in an out-of-balance state are certainly likely to damage project outcomes.

Balance also carries the idea of nonlinearity in the framework, meaning that though you may attempt to follow the ideal chain of inquiry from left to right, you won't know all information at any given point in a project. That, however, cannot prevent you from moving the project forward. The longer you go without critical data, the more likely you will need to revisit the core project goals repeatedly, with significant costs.

Breaking the Chain

The concept of balance serves to remind you, as a learning consultant, that all the elements are important and that you face challenges when you break the chain by failing to care for any one element. If you fail to build the chain by planning for leading forces or fail to balance the chain by caring for emergent forces, the chain can break and you are unlikely to achieve your desired learning and performance results.

A broken chain can occur as one significant event. For example, you don't push back when the client adds two extra review cycles during production, thereby jeopardizing the rollout date. Or it can occur as a compounding issue that remains unaddressed and becomes increasingly larger as the project continues. For example, the stated organizational goal may be increasing the number of calls a call center employee can resolve within an hour by 20 percent. However, you may notice early in the project that the client often discusses calls in terms of customer satisfaction. Without immediately digging deeper about whether the true desired organizational result has been identified, the project may continue only for you to find out at implementation that customer satisfaction was indeed the true result desired—and this then is information that has come much

Map to Measurement

Since the 1950s, Donald Kirkpatrick's four-level model of evaluation—reaction, learning, behavior, and results—has become a widely adopted standard for measuring training programs' outcomes. (The four levels may have been inspired by psychologist Raymond Katzell, as Jim and Wendy Kirkpatrick note.) More recently, Jack and Patti Phillips' return on investment measure was proposed as a fifth level to demonstrate ultimate value to an organization and to aid in allocating resources.

While there are many instruments, tools, and systems for measurement that align with these levels, consider how they map to this framework. The great benefit of adopting a Results Come First framework is that it makes measurement more straightforward and possible. If you and your client have a clear agreement on the results you wish to achieve together, measurement becomes a process of verifying that those results happen.

Notice that measurement will likely occur chronologically—in the same order as the chain of action—and that each element in the chain will require relatively more time to measure. For example, you can evaluate process results at the close of every status meeting by reviewing the desired results and asking the client to report on satisfaction. Up the chain, measuring learner experience results requires a significant number of learners to pass through the complete experience before you can ask them to evaluate it. Ultimately, it may take months—at least a full quarter—for data on organizational results to be reported.

Note: A case could be made for including ROI in the process results and organizational results elements. Though the connection is not as clear, if you and your client use projected ROI to make decisions about which products to create or whether you should create a given product, that does fall clearly into the process results element. However, because such data-driven, collaborative decision making occurs in few cases, it is not depicted here.

Figure 2. Evaluation vs. Results

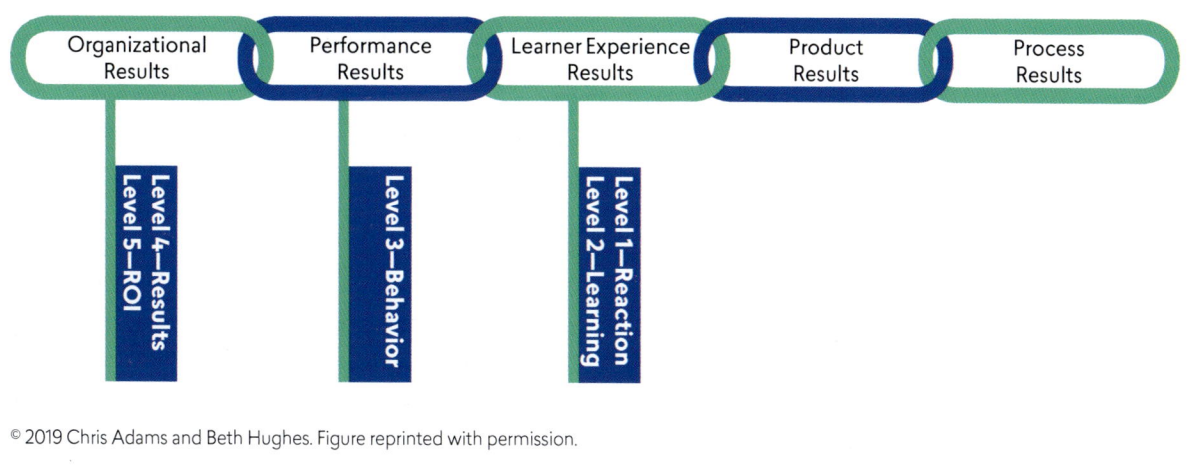

© 2019 Chris Adams and Beth Hughes. Figure reprinted with permission.

too late to enable you to course-correct. Your ability to identify forces that arise and act to maintain the framework balance is a key differentiator between an instructional designer focused on delivering a product and a learning consultant focused on delivering results.

Finally, notice that the framework's balancing point is the learner experience element—the point where the process and product, which are inputs, tip over into performance and organizational results, which are outputs.

The Framework in Action

Applying the Results Come First framework to a critical learning initiative provides an example of how the Results Come First approach can have a real impact on business outcomes. In 2018, a leading content provider in the financial industry needed to renovate its library of sales and service e-learning courses. The stated goals in the request were to retain current clients and gain new ones, attain a competitive edge in the marketplace, and reduce overall learner time. We applied the framework to the request to specify desired results up front and then to maintain a focus on and balance of desired results throughout the project, which led to measurable success with the delivered learning program. Specifically, applying the framework within this training project achieved these results in each element:

- **Process results.** We provided value to the client by gathering data from relationship managers, customers, and the marketing team during analysis to gain insights on perceptions of current training, culture, and openness to innovation. Partnering with the client project team in an iterative design and prototype process resulted in reduced production time with fewer revisions. We built new capabilities in the internal project team to design and develop content under a narrative-based instructional model. Additionally, our focus on value-add development strategies improved the learner experience while managing client requirements, such as budget and timeline.
- **Product results.** We designed and developed 28 three- to five-minute animated microlearning videos and supplemental materials accessible on demand through any available device. Application videos provide fun and engaging practice opportunities with meaningful feedback from a reputable source. We also developed a coaching program to support learning as a process, rather than an event, that any designated coach can deliver in any financial institution or that motivated, self-driven learners can tap.
- **Learning experience results.** This work drove us to define the concept of binge-worthy training materials—or training programs so compelling that learners want to keep taking them. Linked, narrative-driven microlearning videos engaged learners, who became invested in the characters and their stories. Highly engaging application opportunities—such as choose your own adventures—are interactive, comprehensive, and adaptive, contributing to the buzz that the experience generated.
- **Performance results.** We provided context and relevance to sales and service skills for learners using a narrative-based instructional model to tell compelling banking stories. Behavior change increased as a result of our focus on pure, elemental concepts, paired with tools for job transfer and building expertise.
- **Organizational results.** We developed a cutting-edge, marketable product that provided a means for our client's sales team to generate excitement about the offering to current subscribers and new clients. We increased the library's value by providing the same amount of content in 80 percent less learner time in a format much more acceptable to current audiences.

> **The longer consultants go without critical data, the more likely they will need to revisit the core project goals repeatedly, with significant costs.**

Completing the learning project within the Results Come First framework resulted in a product that met the client's and stakeholders' initially stated goals. It also identified and met additional business and performance goals that were initially unknown. Through the process of guiding our client's focus on results, we were able to help the client's thinking evolve from a product request to an outcome aligned with the business as a whole. As a result, we created an effective learning experience that positively affected the company's sales and customer relationships.

Conclusion

The Results Come First framework is not a new idea. At its most basic, it's a restatement of the principle behind American educator and author Stephen Covey's second habit of his 7 *Habits of Highly Effective People*, "Begin with the end in mind." Similarly, in his foundational work on needs assessment, Roger Kaufman, professor emeritus at Florida State University, stressed a focus on *ends* before *means*. Most approaches to the measurement of learning outcomes (such as those put forth by Donald Kirkpatrick, industrial-organizational psychologist Raymond Katzell, and Jack and Patti Phillips in their return-on-investment model) encourage establishing desired results as a prerequisite for measurement. Further, many models link the performance of people to business results.

With this results-first concept, we seek to promote a clear and constant focus on results through this framework as a pervasive and guiding principle to your work as a learning consultant. This framework is a differentiating characteristic that divides the roles of instructional designer and learning consultant and sets apart the most successful learning consultants.

For learning professionals, the pressure to simply deliver solutions has never been greater. We believe that an ever-stronger focus on results is needed for you—and HR, organizational development, and other talent-centered professionals—to effectively contribute to an organization's success. *Results first* is easy to say but difficult to achieve in practice. However, it is a principle that must be continually and loudly championed. The framework is meant to be adaptable to whatever process or context in which you choose to apply it. That means you can try it immediately. But before you do, consider what results you hope to achieve.

References & Resources

Books

Brethower, D., and K. Smalley. 1998. *Performance-Based Instruction.* San Francisco, CA: Jossey-Bass/Pfeiffer.

Clark, R.C. 2014. *Evidence-Based Training Methods: A Guide for Training Professionals.* Alexandria, VA: ASTD Press.

Gilbert, T.F. 2007. *Human Competence: Engineering Worthy Performance.* San Francisco, CA: Pfeiffer.

Kaufman, R., and I. Guerra-López. 2013. *Needs Assessment for Organizational Success.* Alexandria, VA: ASTD Press.

Kirkpatrick, D., and J. Kirkpatrick. 2006. *Evaluating Training Programs: The Four Levels.* San Francisco, CA: Berrett-Koehler.

Knowles, M.S., E.F. Holton III, and R.A. Swanson. 2015. *The Adult Learner: The Definitive Classic in Adult Education and Human Resource Development.* Abington, UK: Routledge.

Obrist, H.U. 2014. *Ways of Curating.* New York, NY: Farrar, Straus and Giroux.

Phillips, J. 2012. *Handbook of Training Evaluation and Measurement Methods.* Abington, UK: Routledge.

Robinson, D.G., and J.C. Robinson. 1998. *Moving From Training to Performance: A Practical Guidebook.* San Francisco, CA: Berrett-Koehler.

Robinson, D.G., J.C. Robinson, J. Phillips, P. Phillips, and D. Handshaw. 2015. *Performance Consulting: A Strategic Process to Improve, Measure, and Sustain Organizational Results.* San Francisco, CA: Berrett-Koehler.

Rummler, G.A., and A.P. Brache. 1995. *Improving Performance: How to Manage the White Space on the Organization Chart. The Jossey-Bass Management Series.* San Francisco, CA: Jossey-Bass.

Articles

Kirkpatrick, J., and W. Kirkpatrick. 2018. "Newly Discovered Article from 1956 Reveals a Four Levels Surprise." Kirkpatrick Partners, January 31. www.kirkpatrickpartners.com/blog/id/843/newly-discovered-article-from-1956-reveals-a-four-levels-surprise.

Thalheimer, W. 2018. "Donald Kirkpatrick Was NOT the Originator of the Four-Level Model of Learning Evaluation." Work-Learning Research, January 30. www.worklearning.com/2018/01/30/donald-kirkpatrick-was-not-the-originator-of-the-four-level-model-of-learning-evaluation.

Job Aid

Results Come First Glossary

Use this glossary—even post it where you can see it regularly—to maintain a focus on results coming first, with an emphasis on the learner experience.

Term	Definition
Results	These are the outcomes—what stakeholders involved in a project or initiative wish to achieve through their investment of time, money, and energy. Results occur as the outcome of any action or inaction. Desired results should be agreed upon as early as possible to produce intended outcomes and avoid wasted effort.
Framework	This is the conceptual framework that links elements together.
Element	This is the top-level organizing components of the framework. The Results Come First framework is comprised of five elements: organizational results, performance results, learner experience results, product results, and process results.
Chain of inquiry	This is the movement through the framework elements from left to right early in a project to discover desired results for each element. Elements are chained in that results for each successive element are those required to enable the current element's results. For instance, the learning consultant may ask, "What performance is required to produce the desired organizational results?"
Chain of action	This is the movement through the framework elements from right to left over the course of a project to enact each element. Like the chain of inquiry, elements are chained in that action in each element produces the next element. For instance, employing a process results in products, and implementing those products produces a learner experience.
Leading forces	These are forces that exist at the beginning of a project and that are likely to exert pressure on one or more elements, sending results out of balance.
Emergent forces	These are forces that emerge during the course of a project and that are likely to exert pressure on one or more elements, sending results out of balance.
Weight of focus	This is intentional thought and action applied to framework elements to counterbalance leading and emergent forces and keep results in balance.
Balance	This is the state when all elements of the framework are cared for, all forces are balanced, work proceeds smoothly, and desired results are produced.
Factors	These are the sublevel organizing components of the framework. Each element includes corresponding factors.

Job Aid

Results-Focused Questions Bank

To identify desired results, learning consultants need to complete a results analysis. To gather the information needed, ask leaders, business partners, stakeholders, and clients questions that are targeted to identify their desired outcomes for each framework element. This bank of questions is designed to help you identify desired results. Use the questions to help you plan meetings and conversations with clients and other stakeholders, selecting the most appropriate questions and adding some of your own. You will likely spread the questions across your entire analysis phase rather than asking them all at once, and although they are organized according to the chain of inquiry here, you can ask them in whatever order works best for your project.

Organizational Results

What measurable business results would you like to achieve (such as cost, revenue, compliance)?

What does success look like?

What are the risks if the organizational goals aren't met?

What organizational goals or factors are most important to you?

What barriers do you see to achieving the desired business results?

Performance Results

Goals

What goals or metrics exist for the targeted employees for the training program?

What goals or targeted metrics exist for the general employee population?

What is the desired performance you would like to see of employees as a result of this program (such as behavior change, time to proficiency)?

What performance goals or factors are most important to you?

What barriers do you see to achieving the desired performance?

Measurement

How do employees know how well they are performing?

How do employees know how they are expected to perform?

What do you think would help employees be more successful at their jobs?

How are employees evaluated on training?

Learning Experience Results

Culture

What is the typical experience that employees have with your current training program?

What feedback have you heard about existing training programs? What typically works well, and what could be improved?

How are employees currently onboarded through HR and on their teams? Are these processes aligned?

How often and under what circumstances do employees typically take training courses (such as annual requirements, self-motivated to increase skills and knowledge, required by management, new hire, change of position)?

Do employees have access to coaches or mentors?

Is there anything about your work environment that would limit learners' ability to take training courses if they were delivered in various ways?

Where do employees go if they have a question on the job?

Expectations

What expectations do employees have of training programs?

What would make learners more likely to take training courses if they weren't required?

What is the desired learning experience you would like employees to have (such as acceptance, engagement, promotion)?

What learning experience goals or factors are most important to you?

Are there any barriers to providing the desired learning experience?

Job Aid

Results-Focused Questions Bank (Cont.)

Motivation

How do managers support learning and professional development?

What motivates employees and provides incentives for them to excel at their jobs?

What happens when employees make a mistake or perform poorly?

Product Results

Audience

What is the average age range of your employees?
- ☐ 24 or younger ☐ 25-34 ☐ 35-44
- ☐ 45-54 ☐ 55-64 ☐ 65 or older

What is the average level of education of your employees?
- ☐ High school ☐ Some college
- ☐ Associate's degree ☐ Bachelor's degree
- ☐ Advanced degree

How long have employees typically been with the company? In their role?

What is your turnover rate?

What languages should the product account for?

What disabilities, challenges, or individual factors should the product account for?

Environment

Which media formats are audience members familiar with (such as live, video, web, mobile)?

What type of training do employees typically prefer?

How will this new program be marketed to audience members and stakeholders?

What product goals or factors are most important to you?

What other initiatives are occurring that may affect the training program?

Are there any barriers to producing products aligned with these desired results?

Delivery Systems

How do learners access learning?

How does the organization track learning and professional development? How are employees held accountable?

How will updates to existing courses be deployed, and how will learners register?

How are technology users supported in your organization?

What support issues are most frequently reported?

Tasks

What training is currently available for the targeted group of employees? What is required?

What other training programs exist? What formats exist, how were they created, and who delivers them?

What tasks should targeted employees be able to complete after the training courses?

Process Results

What's your current process from training program development to implementation?

What terminology do you use to name the parts of your existing learning products (such as courses, units, modules, lessons)?

What are some success and risk factors based on previous training initiatives?

What process goals or factors are most important to you?

Are there any barriers to following a process designed to achieve these results?

Is it time to move away from a linear approach to instructional design?

Use the LLAMA™ methodology, based on the Agile project management approach, to design content that learners truly need.

Available at td.org/books/agile